☐ will sympathise

☐ will laugh at

Without her friendship I would be

☐ as sad as the Saddest Thing in Sad Land

☐ would eat much, much more chocolate.

And so I promise ☐ to call her occasionally

☐ promise her my total and

undying friendship.

Signed......................................

Date...

Other giftbooks in this series

Birthday Girl!
Birthday Boy!
Sorry
Little things mean a lot
Go Girl!
I love you madly

Published in 2007 by Helen Exley Giftbooks in Great Britain.
Illustrations by Caroline Gardner © Caroline Gardner Publishing 2005
Illustrations by Roger Greenhough © Helen Exley 2007
All illustrations are based on the Caroline Gardner Elfin range
Text, selection and arrangement © Helen Exley 2007
The moral right of the author has been asserted.

12 11 10 9 8 7 6 5 4 3 2
ISBN 13: 978-1-84634-095-6

Words by Stuart and Linda Macfarlane
Edited by Helen Exley
Pictures by Caroline Gardner and Roger Greenhough
Printed in China
Helen Exley Giftbooks, 16 Chalk Hill, Watford, Herts WD19 4BG, UK
www.helenexleygiftbooks.com

Funny little people...

My friend

By Stuart &
Linda Macfarlane

A HELEN EXLEY GIFTBOOK

A friend is
someone who has
the patience of a saint,
the strength of an army
and half your CD collection.

It's your imperfections that

A good friend is
like a one-eyed teddy bear;
soft, comforting and gentle
– but never perfect.

nake you the perfect friend.

Friend: someone who willingly lends you her best clothes.
And also has a very bad memory.

It's good to have friends – you always

have someone to blame.

Silence: the period of time when a friend is not talking – measured in microseconds.

Friend: a person whose phone bill exceeds her income.

You can always
    depend on a friend
to get you out of a tough situation
– well at least
    the ones she created.

When they immediately reply "yes", before knowing what you need, you know you have a friend.

You know she's a great friend if...
After spending the day together
she phones you for a chat.
She's training for a marathon because
you want to run one.
She doesn't buy the dress you're
considering buying.
She sends you postcards when
you are on holiday.
She puts her birthday into your diary.

When I awake my
first thoughts are of her
– my best friend.
What shall we do today?
Where shall we go?
What trouble
will she get me into?

Friend: someone who is kind, considerate, thoughtful, loving, selfless, caring and very probably a little bit mad!

If I had to choose
between a weekend with you
or a skiing trip...
I would definitely
send you a postcard.

A friend may not
always be able
to stop your tears,
but she will
always be there
with a box of tissues.

...and then I
noticed this person at the party
wearing really silly shoes.
Her hair was like a bird's nest.
Immediately I knew
Miss Odd Shoes
would become my friend.
"Perfect" I thought.

My friend and I
have little need for words.
We can read each other's expressions,
interpret every subtle nuance.
This of course does not stop us chatting
for hour after hour
after hour.

A good friend

is someone who

only tells you

that your idea

was insane after

you've both

made the

parachute jump.

A friend
is just a stranger
who is yet to take over your life,
and borrow your best clothes.

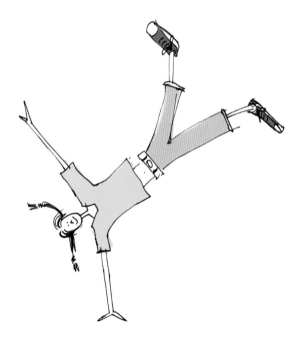

My friend can climb Everest
with her eyes shut!
My friend can slay dragons
with her bare hands!
My friend can swim the Atlantic
with her legs tied together!
My friend can do anything...
well perhaps not,
but she always makes me laugh
when I'm feeling blue.

Friends! Who needs them?
They seldom call you
when they say they will.
Not always there
when you need them most.
Quite probably forget your birthday.
May even let you down.
But I never claimed to be perfect….
So – give me one more chance!!

You are always
a little kinder than
you have to be.
Always a little more helpful.
You don't just
go the extra mile
– you do the whole marathon.

For you I would do anything
– yes, absolutely anything.
I would give up boys for a year.
I would dye my hair green.
I would deprive myself
of chocolate and muffins.
I would gladly do these things
and more.... But please don't ask!!

Never feel
the need to
say "sorry" to me.
Grovelling
is quite enough.

You can trust a good friend
to be completely honest
about everything –
except your wrinkles,
your drooping tummy,
your bum size....

A friend is
someone you phone when
you find a spider in the bath.
They may not rush round to help
but at least you can
scream together.

A good friend
helps you choose the
best paths through life
but a great friend
drives you there.

It's easy to spot good friends.
As they stroll together
their strides are in perfect unison
as if walking to the beat
of a common tune. Each action,
each smile, each nod,
each gesture, each overdraft
in union as if linked.

Some friends
like the same foods...
Enjoy the same movies.
Like the same clothes.
Share the same hobbies
...fight over the same guys.

You may not be
a computer whiz
but, goodness, somehow you
manage to send me
twenty emails a day.

I'm receiving more and
more junk email every day
– most of it's from you!

For the time
she fell off the bus seat,
for the time she wore a
pair of woolly tights
in place of her scarf;
for sometimes looking
like a stray cat...

I love her dearly, my scatty friend.

She's all the friends

I ever need.

And so you have to
go again and
leave me all alone.
This is my darkest hour.
See you tomorrow!

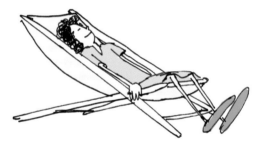

My friend and I
can spend a day doing nothing
and saying very little
but still have
a wonderful time.

Thanks –
For never criticizing
my awful choice of guys.
For putting up with
my many tantrums.
For always being there
when I really need you.
For giving advice when I want it
and keeping quiet when I don't.
For being the world's
greatest friend.
– Thanks.

A crowded room,
Anonymous faces,
Strangers.
A single word,
A smile,
A friend.

What is important
is that you have one real friend
– someone you can
completely trust,
someone who's there on
all the very ordinary days.

When I'm not with her I'm

ke a polar bear in a desert.

Friendship is
the greatest gift one person
can give to another.

She is the glue that holds my

world together.

I'm not strong.
She's not strong.
But together
my friend and I
make the strongest force
in the known universe.

Helen Exley runs her own publishing company
which sells giftbooks in more than seventy countries.
Helen's books cover the many events and emotions in life,
and she was eager to produce a book to say a simple "sorry".
Caroline Gardner's delightfully quirky "elfin" cards
provided the inspiration Helen needed to go ahead
with this idea, and from there this series of stylish
and witty books quickly grew.

Caroline Gardner Publishing has been producing beautifully
designed stationery from offices overlooking the River Thames
in England since 1993 and has been developing the distinctive
"elfin" stationery range over the last five years.
There are also several new illustrations created especially for
these books by artist Roger Greenhough.

Stuart and Linda Macfarlane live in Glasgow, Scotland.
They have produced several books with Helen Exley
including *The Little Book of Stress*, *Old Wrecks' Jokes*,
and the hugely successful *Utterly adorable cats*.